JAMES *Madison*

Our PRESIDENTS

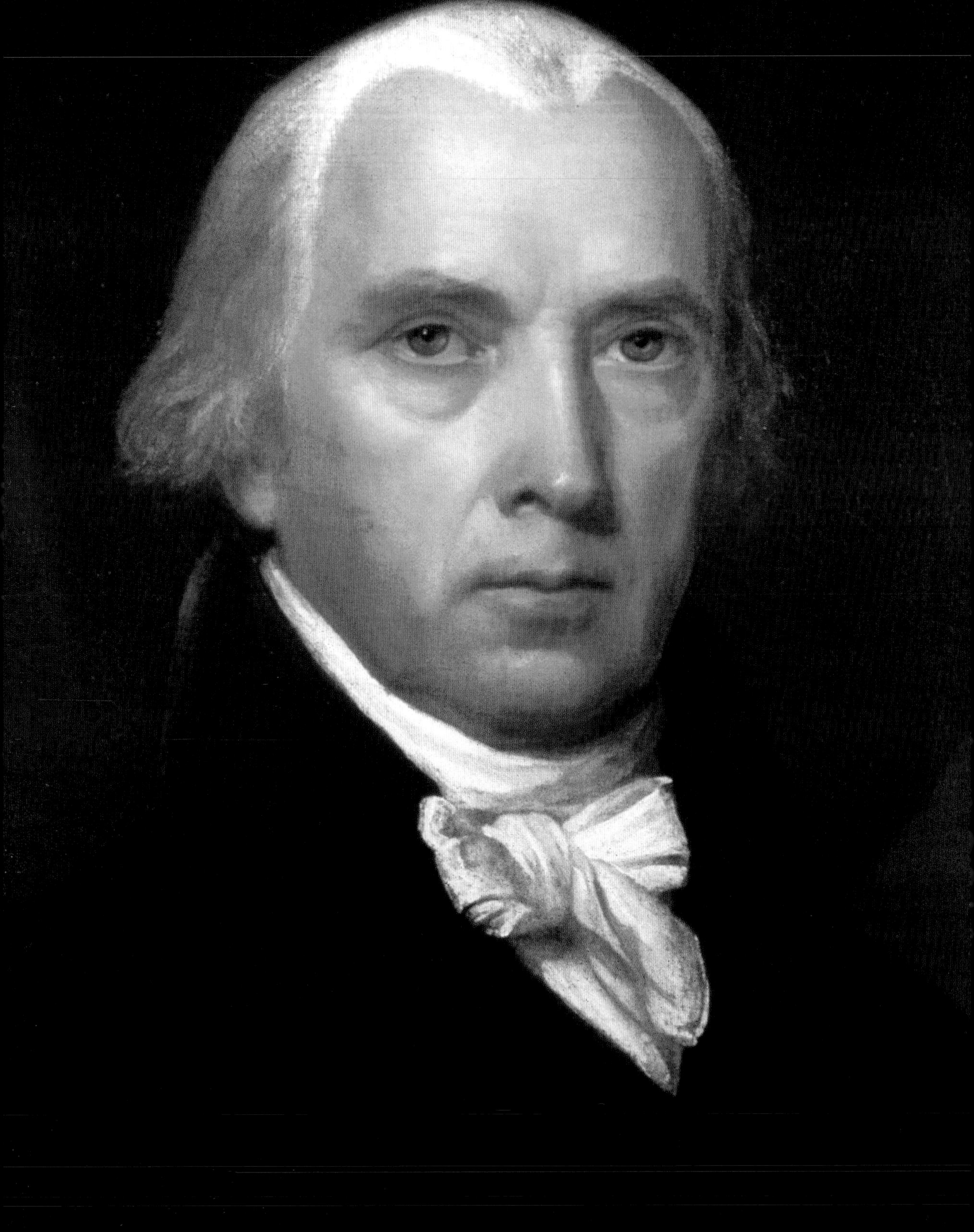

JAMES *Madison*

OUR FOURTH PRESIDENT

By Ann Graham Gaines

SPIRIT
of America™

The Child's World®, Inc.
Chanhassen, Minnesota

6

JAMES *Madison*

Published in the United States of America by The Child's World®, Inc.
PO Box 326 • Chanhassen, MN 55317-0326 • 800-599-READ • www.childsworld.com

Acknowledgments
The Creative Spark: Mary Francis-DeMarois, Project Director; Elizabeth Sirimarco Budd, Series Editor; Robert Court, Design and Art Direction; Janine Graham, Page Layout; Jennifer Moyers, Production

The Child's World®, Inc.: Mary Berendes, Publishing Director; Red Line Editorial, Fact Research; Cindy Klingel, Curriculum Advisor; Robert Noyed, Historical Advisor

Photos
Cover: White House Collection, courtesy White House Historical Association; Belle Grove Plantation, Middletown, VA: 7, 33; The Free Library of Philadelphia, The Print and Picture Collection: 24; Independence National Historical Park: 6, 14, 15, 16; Library of Congress Collection: 10, 21 (retouching courtesy of David M. Budd Photography), 27, 29, 31; The Library of Virginia: 12; Courtesy of Montpelier National Trust: 19, 22; Courtesy of the Museum of American History: 35; Princeton University Library: 8-9; ©Collection of the New-York Historical Society: 32; Stock Montage: 20, 23; Virginia Historical Society: 34

Registration
The Child's World®, Inc., Spirit of America™, and their associated logos are the sole property and registered trademarks of The Child's World®, Inc.

Library of Congress Cataloging-in-Publication Data
Gaines, Ann.
  James Madison : our fourth president / by Ann Graham Gaines.
    p. cm.
  ISBN 1-56766-840-2 (alk. paper)
  1. Madison, James, 1751–1836—Juvenile literature. 2. Presidents—United States—
Biography—Juvenile literature. [1. Madison, James, 1751–1836. 2. Presidents.] I. Title.
E342 .G25 2001
  973.5'1'092—dc21

00-010572

Contents

Chapter ONE   *A Thoughtful Leader*   6

Chapter TWO   *Father of the Constitution*   14

Chapter THREE   *A New War*   22

Chapter FOUR   *Honored Leader*   32

Time Line   36

Glossary Terms   38

Our Presidents   42

Presidential Facts   46

For Further Information   47

Index   48

A Thoughtful Leader

James Madison was president of the United States for just eight years, but he worked for almost half a century to keep the nation strong and united.

JAMES MADISON, BORN ON MARCH 16, 1751, was the oldest in a family of 12 children. The Madisons lived on what was then the **frontier** in the colony of Virginia. They owned a large tobacco **plantation** called Montpelier (mont-PEEL-yur). Like other planters, James Madison's father owned many slaves, who labored in his fields and mansion.

James was often sick when he was a boy and had to stay inside most of the time. Doctors said something was wrong with his liver. He also had what he called "falling sickness," which was probably **epilepsy.** Sometimes he collapsed with frightening **seizures.**

There was no school near Montpelier, so Mr. and Mrs. Madison taught their children at home. The family owned many books. James had read all of them by the time he was 11 years old. Then his parents sent him away to attend a boarding school. When he was 16, his father hired a tutor to teach the Madison children at home. James was then able to return to Montpelier to take his lessons.

In 1769, James Madison enrolled at the College of New Jersey (later renamed Princeton University). He hungered for knowledge and learning but still found time for fun. He and his friends liked to play pranks and talk in their rooms until late at night. They had conversations about all kinds of things, but their favorite subject was **politics.** Around that time, England had ordered colonists to pay new taxes, but they would not allow Americans to have a **representative** in the English government. Madison and his friends believed this was unfair. Many colonists shared this opinion.

James Madison's father, who was also named James, was a successful planter and a wealthy citizen.

It usually took students four years to finish their college studies. Madison studied so hard, he finished in just two years. But all this effort was not without its price. Madison became so sick that he could not attend his graduation. Then he had to stay in New Jersey for one whole year before he felt well enough to travel back to Virginia. The year was not unhappy, though, for Madison spent his time doing the

8

things he liked best—reading, writing, and talking. When his friends came to visit, they still discussed politics. The colonies teetered at the edge of a **revolution,** and Madison believed Americans should fight for independence from England.

Madison finally returned to Montpelier in 1772. He took over the task of teaching his brothers and sisters and studied law books

Interesting Facts

▶ During his second year at college, Madison slept only five hours a night so he would have enough time for all of his studies.

When Madison returned to Montpelier, he was 21 years old. He was full grown but remained short and pale, and he was not very strong. Madison still worked with his father on the plantation, though. He helped choose which crops to grow and where to sell them. His interest in politics was growing, too. In just a few years, at the age of 25, young Madison would help create Virginia's constitution.

in his spare time. Madison never became a lawyer, but he did use what he learned from those books. The information helped him understand how to present a good argument. Once he used his law training to help a group of ministers who had been sent to jail. They were punished for preaching their own views instead of what the Church of England told them to say. James Madison believed in religious freedom, which meant people should be able to practice religion in any way they wanted. He would support this **ideal** all his life.

According to the laws of the day, only landowners could vote and run for office. Madison bought land in 1774 so he could vote. Soon he decided to play a role in the government. The county voters elected him to the Committee of Safety. This was the group of people the town put in charge of preparing for war with England. Madison also joined the **militia.** The Revolutionary War finally broke out in 1775, and Madison wanted to join the army as a soldier. Unfortunately, he still wasn't healthy enough for such a life. Even so, he would make important contributions to the revolutionary effort.

Americans from each colony had to decide if they truly wanted independence. In May of 1776, Madison attended the Virginia Revolutionary **Convention.** The people at this meeting sent a message to the **Continental Congress,** telling its members to vote for independence. They also wrote a new **constitution** for Virginia. Madison remained a shy young man, but he had begun to speak out much more in public. He often stood up at these meetings to explain quietly but firmly what he thought the constitution should say. He wrote the section of the Virginia constitution that guaranteed religious freedom. Madison was not one to boast, but he did say how proud he was to have helped create that important **document.**

In 1777, Madison was asked to join the Governor's Council. He became friends with Thomas Jefferson, who was also a member of the council. Jefferson and Madison shared many interests. They both loved to read,

Madison lived at his childhood home, Montpelier (above), throughout much of his adult life, but his involvement in American government meant that he often had to leave home.

write, and talk about ideas. In 1779, Madison was elected to the Continental Congress. He soon became known as a great thinker who could solve problems.

Madison remained in Congress after the Revolution. By then, the new nation was governed by the **Articles of Confederation.** He thought this document was a terrible plan because it gave the states more power than the **federal** government had. Madison and other leaders wanted to find a way to make the nation's government stronger.

They worried that without a united leadership, the country might fall apart.

Madison's term in Congress ended in 1783. He went home to Montpelier, but he would not stay there for long. The new nation needed its brightest leaders to help decide its fate. In 1784, Madison was elected to the Virginia legislature, the group of people who made the state's laws. He left Montpelier for the state capital of Richmond. There he realized that the 13 states were having trouble cooperating. Representatives from each state argued about **commerce,** and this worried Madison. In 1785, he suggested that **delegates** from every state meet to talk about the problems they were having.

At the first commerce meeting, the delegates decided that the states needed more than new **trade** agreements. Perhaps the Articles of Confederation needed to be completely changed. The delegates scheduled a convention to start in Philadelphia on May 14, 1787. When it began, the delegates decided the Articles of Confederation could not be fixed. They voted to replace them with a new constitution.

Chapter TWO

Father of the Constitution

Madison took notes each day at the Constitutional Convention. Then he stayed up late at night to recopy them, although he said it "nearly killed" him. He wanted to preserve a record of this important event, and his notes contributed much of what we know today about the convention.

JAMES MADISON WAS AN IMPORTANT LEADER at the Constitutional Convention. In fact, he played such a big role that he is often called "The Father of the Constitution." Even before he got to Philadelphia, Madison had thought a lot about how a government should work. He was prepared to tell the delegates what he believed the Constitution should say. Shy Mr. Madison managed to give very exciting speeches.

Madison brought a document with him called the Virginia Plan. It said that the delegates from Virginia believed the nation needed a strong central government. It also said the federal government should have more power than the states. The plan became the basis of the Constitution, which established

a federal government with three parts—the **executive,** the **judicial,** and the **legislative** branches. Madison also suggested the system of **checks and balances,** which made sure that none of the three branches could have too much power.

The convention delegates argued for months. They finally adopted the Constitution on September 17, 1787. Then it had to be accepted by the states. It took a long time, but the Constitution was **ratified** the following year. Many ideas in the document were those of James Madison.

George Washington was named chairman of the Constitutional Convention, and he worked hard to make the delegates listen to each other. Sometimes they had terrible arguments, but finally they agreed on what the Constitution should say. This did not make it official, however. Now the states had to ratify it.

While Thomas Jefferson was in France, he sent Madison books about various forms of government. This information proved helpful as Madison helped craft the Constitution. The two men would remain friends for the rest of their lives.

Once the Constitution was ratified, a new federal government was created with a president, a vice president, and a new Congress. James Madison was elected a member of the House of Representatives, which met in New York, the nation's capital at the time. He was a leader in Congress. Other politicians had developed a deep respect for this quiet thinker with the small voice and big ideas. He proposed the first **departments** of the federal government. These dealt with issues of war, **finance,** and **foreign affairs.** He introduced the act that created a national court system. But he fought hardest for the **Bill of Rights.** He introduced those **amendments** to the Constitution on June 8, 1789.

While Madison was serving in Congress, Thomas Jefferson returned to the United States from France. He had spent the last five years there as a **diplomat.** Madison and Jefferson had written to each other often while

Jefferson was away. They were pleased that they could finally talk face-to-face. By 1792, the nation's politicians had divided into two **political parties.** Jefferson and Madison led the **Republican Party** (also called the Democratic-Republican Party). They often argued angrily with members of the **Federalist Party,** led by Alexander Hamilton. Madison remained soft-spoken, but he was now used to public speaking.

One thing the two parties argued about was what sort of relations the United States should have with France and England. The French had their own revolution, removing the nation's king from power. Now they wanted to overthrow other governments that were led by kings and queens. They even declared war on England. Madison and many other Republicans thought Americans should fight with France because they had signed an agreement saying they would. Federalists wanted to side with England. But President Washington decided the United States should remain **neutral.**

During this time, James Madison made a change in his personal life. In 1794, he

Interesting Facts

▸ Madison worked with Alexander Hamilton to write *The Federalist Papers,* a series of essays written to convince the states to ratify the Constitution. Later, however, the two men would become bitter political enemies.

▸ James Madison and Thomas Jefferson created a code so they could write secret letters to one another.

▸ James Madison took the floor to speak at the Constitutional Convention 200 times.

▸ Dolley Madison's father was a farmer who hated slavery. He finally freed his slaves, which made it impossible to run his farm. He had to sell his land and move his wife and nine children to a small house in Philadelphia.

▸ As an adult, James Madison was against slavery, but he still used the slaves he inherited from his father. When he moved to Philadelphia to take his seat in the Continental Congress, he took a slave along to work for him.

married a widow named Dolley Payne Todd. Dolley was a friendly and energetic woman, and Madison loved her deeply.

Madison remained intensely involved in politics until George Washington left office at the end of his second term. Then Madison retired. He and Dolley moved to Montpelier, where they added rooms and decorated the mansion. But during the presidency of John Adams, Congress passed the **Alien** and **Sedition** Acts. These were used to keep the country safe from spies or dangerous talk against the government. Madison was so angry about these acts, he returned to politics.

There were three Alien Acts. Two of them could be used to make foreigners leave the country, even if they had done nothing wrong. The third act made foreigners wait longer to become American citizens. Madison called this law "a monster."

Madison hated the Sedition Act even more. It said Americans could not criticize the government. Madison thought this was danger-ous. He explained why in a paper he wrote called "The Virginia Resolves." He argued that the Acts were unconstitutional, which meant

Dolley Madison was a bright, charming woman who was famous for the parties she gave. When Thomas Jefferson became president, Dolley often acted as the White House hostess for him because his wife had died many years earlier.

that they ignored the laws of the Constitution. The Sedition Act, for example, took away Americans' freedom of speech, even though the Bill of Rights guaranteed it.

Madison thought the Alien and Sedition Acts threatened the Constitution and even the country itself. When John Adams ran for a second term in 1800, Madison fought against his reelection. He wanted to be sure a Federalist would not lead the country, so he helped his good friend Thomas Jefferson become the nation's third president.

IN 1794, JAMES MADISON married a widow named Dolley Payne Todd. He was 43, and she was 26. Dolley Madison had been raised in the Quaker religion. This meant not only that she went to Quaker meetings—or church services—but also that she wore only plain clothes and could not go to parties or dances. But after her first husband died, Dolley stopped following Quaker ways. She started buying fancy clothes, and she especially loved hats. In Washington, D.C., she became a popular hostess. In fact, it was Dolley who established the role that future first ladies would play in their husbands' careers. She threw exciting parties that people loved to attend. Her guests liked to listen to her smart and witty discussions. She always had something to say, and she laughed a lot. Dolley was six inches taller than her husband. Compared to her, Madison seemed especially small and quiet. Nevertheless, he always appreciated her lively qualities.

Dolley Madison would outlive her husband. After his death, leaders in government kept in touch with her, and first ladies asked her for advice. She decided to return to live in Washington. Although almost 70 by that time, the people of the nation's capital found her just as charming as ever. One of the treasures kept at the Library of Congress is this portrait of her, which is from the very earliest days of photography.

Chapter THREE

A New War

Madison became the secretary of state in 1801, which meant he was in charge of the nation's foreign affairs. He would hold the position for the next eight years.

BY THE TIME JEFFERSON BECAME PRESIDENT, the capital of the United States had moved to Washington, D.C. Jefferson named Madison his secretary of state, which made him an important assistant to the president. In this position, he was in charge of the country's foreign affairs. This would be a difficult job because the United States had problems with both France and England at the time.

France and England wanted to limit America's trade with other countries. For years, the British stopped American ships and made the captains hand over their cargo. Then in June of 1807, a British warship attacked an American ship. The British killed one American sailor and captured three more, claiming that they were British **deserters.**

When Jefferson was president, the British began stopping American ships at sea. They kidnapped U.S. sailors and forced them to join the British navy. This led to the Embargo Act of 1807.

Madison and Jefferson did not want to go to war. They sent diplomats to try to find a solution, but nothing worked.

In December of 1807, Congress passed the **Embargo** Act. It said American ships could not transport goods to England—or to anywhere else in Europe. European ships could not enter American ports either. Jefferson and Madison believed this might force France and England to leave American

A nasty political cartoon from the time of the Embargo Act shows a tiny Madison (at left) copying the actions of Thomas Jefferson. A French leader is shown teasing them.

ships alone. They thought the Europeans would lose money without American goods. Eventually they would want the goods back and agree to stop bothering American ships.

The Embargo Act did hurt France and England, but it made Americans lose money, too. They could not sell the things they made or grew. Grains and other goods spoiled in storage before they could be sold, and farmers lost a lot of money. Sailors and shipbuilders also lost their jobs because American ships were no longer sailing across the Atlantic. Worst of all, **smugglers** were sneaking goods out of the country illegally.

Finally, Congress ended the Embargo Act. In March of 1809, American ships again were allowed to transport goods abroad, but English and French ships were still not allowed to come into American ports.

By this time, another presidential election had taken place. Jefferson did not want to run again, so Madison ran as the Republican **candidate.** In February of 1809, the election results were announced in Congress. Hundreds of people crowded in to hear the news. James Madison had won!

His **inauguration** was held in March on a warm, sunny day. Ten thousand people watched as he took the oath of office in his quiet, calm voice. Then he made a short speech. He swore to uphold peace as long as possible. But he also promised to go to war if the nation was threatened.

That night, he and Dolley threw a fancy ball. On March 11, they moved into the

25

▸ James and Dolley Madison never had any children together, but Dolley had two sons from her first marriage.

▸ Dolley Madison's sister married a Supreme Court justice at the White House. It was the first wedding ever to be held there.

presidential mansion, which Dolley redecorated with satin and velvet curtains and huge mirrors. Washington leaders admired her charm and enjoyed her famous parties. James Madison adored his wife and loved to see her excited and happy, but he was quiet at the parties. He still worried about problems with England. The English continued to stop American ships and kidnap their sailors. Madison wrote many official letters protesting such actions. England still refused to treat the United States fairly.

In the fall of 1811, James and Dolley returned to Washington after a long summer vacation at Montpelier. A new session of Congress started in November. Madison sent a message asking the lawmakers to get ready. He believed war was coming. They agreed and voted to spend money to improve the nation's weak army and navy. They also prepared to buy more weapons and recruit more soldiers and sailors.

Madison sent one last **appeal** to England for peace, but he received no reply. On June 18, 1812, he asked Congress to declare war, and it agreed. At first, the war went badly for the Americans. It seemed almost certain that the

United States would be defeated, and its independence was at risk. America might become part of England again if it lost the war.

Federalists complained about "Mr. Madison's War." They seemed to have forgotten the problems England had caused. But Americans didn't listen to the Federalists.

In 1813, Madison was reelected and entered his second term as president.

During the War of 1812, the U.S.S. Constitution *won more battles than any other American ship. Here it is shown in its victory over the* Guerrière. *Today "Old Ironsides," as the* Constitution *is known, is docked in Boston harbor.*

Then the American navy started to win battles. The greatest victory came on Lake Erie when Captain Oliver Perry captured an entire British squadron. Still, the British kept fighting.

In May of 1814, British ships sailed close to Washington, D.C. Madison knew the city soon would be under attack. When his generals did not do enough to get ready, Madison himself rode out to prepare the army to fight. On August 22, residents of Washington began to flee. Madison ordered that important documents, such as the Declaration of Independence, be moved out of the city and hidden. The president camped with the soldiers. Dolley stayed in the presidential mansion, but she packed the things she loved best, including a valuable painting of President Washington. She prepared to take these items to safety when the British arrived. She used spy glasses to watch other people leave the city. She knew she would soon have

to do the same. On August 23, James went to see Dolley. They did not get to spend much time together. That very night, he received an urgent message: "The enemy are in full march on Washington."

Madison returned to the army the next day. Dolley finally fled the city early that

On August 24, 1814, British forces under the command of Major General Ross seized Washington. Citizens, including the first lady, fled the capital to escape attack.

29

evening, just before the British arrived. Their soldiers went through public buildings, burning furniture and smashing things. At about 10:30, they came to the president's mansion and plundered it, stealing and ruining things as they moved from room to room. Finally, they set fire to it. A big thunderstorm broke over the city the next morning. The rain put out the blaze and many other fires around the city. It also sent the British back to their ships.

From there, the British sailed to Baltimore, where they planned to launch their next attack. But the Americans won an important battle at Fort McHenry, which was built to guard the city of Baltimore. At the same time, American ships won another victory on Lake Champlain. Madison sent representatives to England, hoping to convince the English king to end the war. Finally, a peace treaty was signed on December 24, 1814. But soldiers in America did not know about the treaty, so they fought on. Future president Andrew Jackson won a final battle in New Orleans. Soon after, news of peace arrived from Europe. The war was officially over.

ONE OF THE SADDEST moments in American history occurred on August 24, 1814. British troops marched into Washington, D.C. They wanted to injure Americans' pride, so they planned to destroy the nation's capital. A spy told them which buildings belonged to the federal government. They went from one building to another, destroying them. Finally, they reached the presidential mansion. The soldiers walked in the front door. Everyone had run away, and there was no one left to keep them out of the mansion.

Dolley Madison and her servants had planned a large dinner party before they realized how close the British were. The meal had been cooked and was waiting on the table for the American guests who never came. Instead, the British soldiers took advantage of the situation. They sat down and devoured the feast. After dinner, they went through the house and stole or destroyed many beautiful things. When they finished wrecking the house, they set it on fire. One witness recalled that "the whole building was wrapt in flames." Rain put out the fire before the mansion burned completely, but the inside was ruined.

The painting above shows the state of the White House after the fire. When the president and first lady returned, the building was just a shell, and they could not live there. It was fully restored during James Monroe's presidency.

Chapter FOUR

Honored Leader

Madison never stopped working for what he believed. At age 84, he became president of the American Colonization Society, which helped former slaves settle in Africa.

NEWS OF PEACE MADE JAMES MADISON A hero in the eyes of the American people. Later, citizens would remember what a great leader he had been. They praised him for his role in winning the war. They remembered that even when he was criticized, he always wanted Americans to be able to speak freely. The United States had not gained any new land fighting the War of 1812, but it had won respect from other nations. England now treated the United States as an equal.

Madison went home to Montpelier for a little while. The war had made him tired. But soon he and Dolley returned to Washington. He spent the last year and a half of his term helping the nation recover from the war.

James Madison was glad to leave office in 1817, when James Monroe became the fifth president of the United States. Back at Montpelier, Dolley Madison entertained friends and gardened. James Madison experimented with new crops. Sometimes he visited his old friend Thomas Jefferson.

Although he enjoyed having time to devote to his family, friends, and books, his interest in politics never ended. In 1828, South Carolina decided it would not obey certain laws. Madison picked up his pen to explain exactly why the states had to respect the federal government. He still thought Americans should try harder to **preserve** the **Union** than to protect the rights of individual states. In 1829, he helped write a new constitution for Virginia.

Nelly Conway Madison, James Madison's mother, lived until the age of 97. She still lived at Montpelier with her family, who affectionately called her the "Old Lady."

As an old man, Madison suffered from **rheumatism.** His fingers became so twisted, he could hardly hold a pen. But he still dictated letters and notes to Dolley about what had happened at the Constitutional Convention. His mind remained active until the very end. He suffered a final illness in the summer of 1836, which resulted in his peaceful death on June 28.

Long after he left public office, James Madison remained a popular figure. People admired him as one of the founding fathers. They remembered that he was president when the nation fought bravely in the War of 1812. Today Americans are still inspired by Madison's final message to his countrymen: "The advice nearest to my heart … is that the Union of the States be cherished." James Madison had devoted his life to keeping the nation strong and united.

Madison seldom left Montpelier after he retired. But in 1829, he traveled to Richmond, Virginia to help write a new constitution for the state. He is shown here speaking at the convention to other state leaders.

DURING THE WAR OF 1812, Fort McHenry was very important because it guarded the entrance to Baltimore harbor. The fort's commander wanted a huge flag to fly over it, one that the enemy could see from afar. Such giant flags were often flown at American forts as a symbol of national pride.

The British went on to Baltimore after they captured Washington, D.C., in August of 1814. They started to bomb Fort McHenry on the morning of September 13. The bombardment continued throughout the rainy night. One person who watched from a ship eight miles away was a lawyer named Francis Scott Key. He was anxious to see if the fort had made it through the night and used a telescope to look for the flag. He saw the huge banner flying. It had been raised as the British retreated. Key was so excited that he immediately wrote a long poem about it. Soon it was set to the tune of a popular song and became what we call "The Star-Spangled Banner." The huge flag goes by the same name and is on display at the Museum of American History in Washington, D.C. It is so large that it has to be hung on a wall two stories high. The photograph above shows the flag just before it was taken down for repairs in 1998.

1751 James Madison is born on March 16 in western Virginia. His parents will have 12 children in all.

1762 James Madison leaves home to go to boarding school.

1767 Madison returns to Montpelier, his family's plantation, to study with a tutor whom his father has hired.

1769 Madison leaves Virginia to attend the College of New Jersey.

1771 Madison finishes college in just two years instead of the four years it takes most students. Unfortunately, he has made himself so sick by studying late into the night that he cannot attend graduation.

1772 In April, Madison goes home to Montpelier. He helps his father run the plantation and teaches his younger brothers and sisters.

1774 Madison buys land from his father, which gives him the right to vote and run for office. He is elected to the local Committee of Safety.

1775 The first battles of the Revolutionary War are fought. Madison is not strong enough to join the army but contributes to the cause in other ways.

1776 Madison attends the Virginia Revolutionary Convention, which writes a constitution for the new state.

1777 Madison joins the Virginia Governor's Council. His lifelong friendship with Thomas Jefferson begins.

1779 Madison is elected to the Second Continental Congress.

1783 When Madison's term in Congress ends, he retires to Montpelier.

1784 Madison returns to politics when he is elected to Virginia's state legislature.

1785 James Madison proposes that delegates from every state meet at a convention to discuss commerce. The delegates decide to meet again in 1787 to change the Articles of Confederation. They will then decide to replace the Articles with a new constitution.

1787 On May 14, the Constitutional Convention opens. The delegates sign the Constitution in September, but it still needs to be ratified by at least nine states.

1788 Nine states ratify the U.S. Constitution.

1789 With the Constitution in place, the new federal government is created. Madison is elected to the House of Representatives. He works successfully to

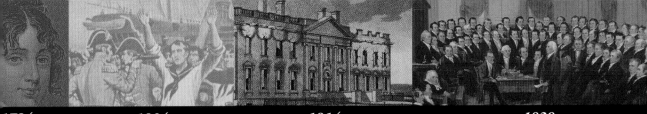
convince other representatives to add amendments to the Constitution, which later become known as the Bill of Rights

1791 The Bill of Rights, which Madison introduced into Congress in 1789, is ratified.

1794 James Madison marries Dolley Payne Todd, a widow.

1797 Madison leaves Congress when President Washington leaves office.

1798 Congress passes the Alien and Sedition Acts, which Madison believes are wrong. He returns to politics to combat what he believes are unconstitutional laws.

1800 Madison helps Thomas Jefferson be elected the third president of the United States. Jefferson names Madison as his secretary of state.

1807 President Jefferson asks Congress to pass the Embargo Act, which stops American trade with European powers. Although the act is meant to hurt England and France, many Americans lose business because of it. The embargo is ended two years later.

1809 James Madison is sworn in as the fourth president of the United States.

1812 The War of 1812 breaks out between England and the United States.

1813 Madison begins his second term as president. The war continues.

1814 On August 24, British troops invade Washington, D.C., and burn many public buildings, including the president's mansion. England finally agrees to peace on December 24, but battles continue in the United States for another month.

1815 On January 8, the Americans beat the British at the Battle of New Orleans.

1817 Madison's term as president ends. He and Dolley return to Montpelier after the new president, James Monroe, is inaugurated.

1828 After South Carolina refuses to obey certain federal laws, Madison again expresses his belief that states must respect the national government.

1829 Madison writes a new constitution for Virginia.

1836 Madison dies on June 28.

37

alien (AY-lee-un)
An alien is a person who is not a citizen of the country where he or she lives. Congress proposed the Alien Acts to keep the country safe from foreign spies.

amendments (uh-MEND-mentz)
Amendments are changes or additions made to the Constitution or other documents. Madison introduced the first amendments to the Constitution (the Bill of Rights).

appeal (uh-PEEL)
An appeal is a serious request for something. Madison sent an appeal to England for peace.

Articles of Confederation (AR-teh-kelz OF kun-fed-uh-RAY-shun)
The Articles of Confederation made up the first plan for a central U.S. government. Many leaders believed the Articles of Confederation did not create a strong enough government.

Bill of Rights (BILL OF RYTZ)
The Bill of Rights are the first 10 amendments to the U.S. Constitution. In the Bill of Rights, Americans are guaranteed basic rights, such as freedom of religion and freedom of speech.

candidate (KAN-deh-dut)
Candidates are people who are running in an election. Several candidates run for president every four years.

checks and balances (CHEKS AND BAL-en-sez)
Checks and balances are the limits the Constitution places on branches of the federal government. For example, the president is commander in chief of the army, but only Congress can declare a war. Checks and balances prevent any one branch from becoming too powerful.

commerce (KOM-urss)
Commerce is the buying and selling of large amounts of goods between different places. Representatives from each state argued about commerce.

constitution (kon-stih-TOO-shun)
A constitution is the set of basic principles that govern a state, country, or society. Madison wrote most of the U.S. Constitution.

Continental Congress (kon-tuh-NEN-tul KONG-gris)
The Continental Congress was the group of men who governed the United States during and after the Revolution. Madison was a member of the Continental Congress.

convention (kun-VEN-shun)
A convention is a meeting. Members of the Constitutional Convention created the U.S. Constitution.

delegates (DEL-eh-getz)
Delegates are people elected to take part in something. Delegates from each state met at the Constitutional Convention to discuss the federal government.

departments (dee-PART-mentz)
Departments are branches within the U.S. government that deal with specific things. The Department of Finance deals with money issues, for example.

deserters (dih-ZER-turz)
Deserters are people who leave something that they shouldn't leave, such as the military. The British searched American ships for deserters from their navy.

diplomat (DIP-luh-mat)
A diplomat is a government official whose job is to represent a country in discussions with other countries. Thomas Jefferson served as a diplomat to France.

document (DOK-yuh-ment)
A document is a written or printed paper that gives people important information. The U.S. Constitution is a document.

embargo (em-BAR-goh)
An embargo stops one country from selling its goods to another country. The United States began an embargo against England in 1807.

epilepsy (ep-uh-LEP-see)
Epilepsy is a disease that affects a person's nervous system. It can cause someone to suffer from seizures and become unconscious.

executive (eg-ZEK-yuh-tiv)
An executive manages things or makes decisions. The executive branch of the U.S. government includes the president and the cabinet members.

federal (FED-ur-ul)
Federal means having to do with the central government of the United States, rather than a state or city government. Madison believed states had to obey federal laws.

**Federalist Party
(FED-ur-ul-ist PAR-tee)**
The Federalist political party in Madison's time was similar to today's Republican Party. Federalists believed that a few well-educated landowners should run the nation.

finance (FY-nanss)
Finance is the management and control of money matters. Madison suggested that a government department should be created to deal with finance.

foreign affairs (FOR-un uh-FAIRZ)
Foreign affairs are matters involving other (foreign) countries. Madison suggested that a government department should be created to deal with foreign affairs.

frontier (frun-TEER)
A frontier is a region that is at the edge of or beyond settled land. As a child, Madison lived on the frontier in western Virginia.

ideal (eye-DEEL)
An ideal is a model or idea of the best something could be. Madison believed in the ideal of religious freedom.

inauguration (ih-naw-gyuh-RAY-shun)
An inauguration is the ceremony that takes place when a new president begins a term. Madison's inauguration was held on March 9, 1809.

judicial (joo-DISH-ul)
Judicial means relating to courts of law. The judicial branch of the federal government includes its courts and judges.

legislative (LEJ-uh-slay-tiv)
Legislative means having to do with the making of laws. The legislative branch of the U.S. government is Congress.

militia (muh-LISH-uh)
A militia is a volunteer army, made up of citizens who have trained as soldiers. Virginia had a militia for times of emergency.

neutral (NOO-trul)
If people are neutral, they do not take sides. President Washington believed the United States should remain neutral in the affairs of other nations.

plantation (plan-TAY-shun)
A plantation is a large farm or group of farms. Montpelier was the name of James Madison's plantation.

political parties (puh-LIT-uh-kul PAR-teez)
Political parties are groups of people who share similar ideas about how to run a government. By 1792, the nation's politicians had begun to divide into political parties.

politics (PAWL-uh-tiks)
Politics refers to the actions and practices of the government. Madison and his college friends talked about politics.

preserve (pree-ZERV)
If people preserve something, they keep it from harm or change. Madison believed Americans should work to preserve the Union.

ratified (RAT-uh-fyd)
If something is ratified, it is approved by a group of people. After the Constitution was written, people from the states ratified it by voting in its favor.

representative (rep-ree-ZEN-tuh-tiv)
A representative is someone who attends a meeting, having agreed to speak or act for others. American colonists believed they should have a representative in the British government.

Republican Party (ree-PUB-lih-ken PAR-tee)
The Republican Party (also called the Democratic-Republican Party) of Madison's time was similar to today's Democratic Party. Members of the party believed that more citizens should be given the right to vote and take part in the federal government.

revolution (rev-uh-LOO-shun)
A revolution is something (such as a war) that causes a complete change in government. The American Revolution was a war fought between the United States and England.

rheumatism (ROO-muh-tih-zim)
Rheumatism is a condition that causes pain in muscles and joints. Madison suffered from rheumatism.

sedition (suh-DIH-shun)
Sedition is something said or written, such as a newspaper article, that causes people to rebel against the government. The Sedition Act said Americans could not criticize government.

seizures (SEE-zhurz)
Seizures are sudden attacks caused by a disease. When people with epilepsy have a seizure, they often collapse, and their bodies make violent jerking motions.

smugglers (SMUG-glerz)
Smugglers are people who illegally bring in or take out something from a country. During the embargo, smugglers took U.S. goods to Britain.

trade (TRAYD)
If two countries (or states) trade with each other, they buy each others' goods. European nations wanted to limit American trade.

union (YOON-yen)
A union is the joining together of two people or groups of people, such as states. The Union is another name for the United States.

Our PRESIDENTS

President	Birthplace	Life Span	Presidency	Political Party	First Lady
George Washington	Virginia	1732–1799	1789–1797	None	Martha Dandridge Custis Washington
John Adams	Massachusetts	1735–1826	1797–1801	Federalist	Abigail Smith Adams
Thomas Jefferson	Virginia	1743–1826	1801–1809	Democratic-Republican	widower
James Madison	Virginia	1751–1836	1809–1817	Democratic Republican	Dolley Payne Todd Madison
James Monroe	Virginia	1758–1831	1817–1825	Democratic Republican	Elizabeth Kortright Monroe
John Quincy Adams	Massachusetts	1767–1848	1825–1829	Democratic-Republican	Louisa Johnson Adams
Andrew Jackson	South Carolina	1767–1845	1829–1837	Democrat	widower
Martin Van Buren	New York	1782–1862	1837–1841	Democrat	widower
William H. Harrison	Virginia	1773–1841	1841	Whig	Anna Symmes Harrison
John Tyler	Virginia	1790–1862	1841–1845	Whig	Letitia Christian Tyler / Julia Gardiner Tyler
James K. Polk	North Carolina	1795–1849	1845–1849	Democrat	Sarah Childress Polk

Our PRESIDENTS

President	Birthplace	Life Span	Presidency	Political Party	First Lady
Zachary Taylor	Virginia	1784–1850	1849–1850	Whig	Margaret Mackall Smith Taylor
Millard Fillmore	New York	1800–1874	1850–1853	Whig	Abigail Powers Fillmore
Franklin Pierce	New Hampshire	1804–1869	1853–1857	Democrat	Jane Means Appleton Pierce
James Buchanan	Pennsylvania	1791–1868	1857–1861	Democrat	never married
Abraham Lincoln	Kentucky	1809–1865	1861–1865	Republican	Mary Todd Lincoln
Andrew Johnson	North Carolina	1808–1875	1865–1869	Democrat	Eliza McCardle Johnson
Ulysses S. Grant	Ohio	1822–1885	1869–1877	Republican	Julia Dent Grant
Rutherford B. Hayes	Ohio	1822–1893	1877–1881	Republican	Lucy Webb Hayes
James A. Garfield	Ohio	1831–1881	1881	Republican	Lucretia Rudolph Garfield
Chester A. Arthur	Vermont	1829–1886	1881–1885	Republican	widower
Grover Cleveland	New Jersey	1837–1908	1885–1889	Democrat	Frances Folsom Cleveland

Our PRESIDENTS

President	Birthplace	Life Span	Presidency	Political Party	First Lady
Benjamin Harrison	Ohio	1833–1901	1889–1893	Republican	Caroline Scott Harrison
Grover Cleveland	New Jersey	1837–1908	1893–1897	Democrat	Frances Folsom Cleveland
William McKinley	Ohio	1843–1901	1897–1901	Republican	Ida Saxton McKinley
Theodore Roosevelt	New York	1858–1919	1901–1909	Republican	Edith Kermit Carow Roosevelt
William H. Taft	Ohio	1857–1930	1909–1913	Republican	Helen Herron Taft
Woodrow Wilson	Virginia	1856–1924	1913–1921	Democrat	Ellen L. Axson Wilson Edith Bolling Galt Wilson
Warren G. Harding	Ohio	1865–1923	1921–1923	Republican	Florence Kling De Wolfe Harding
Calvin Coolidge	Vermont	1872–1933	1923–1929	Republican	Grace Goodhue Coolidge
Herbert C. Hoover	Iowa	1874–1964	1929–1933	Republican	Lou Henry Hoover
Franklin D. Roosevelt	New York	1882–1945	1933–1945	Democrat	Anna Eleanor Roosevelt Roosevelt
Harry S. Truman	Missouri	1884–1972	1945–1953	Democrat	Elizabeth Wallace Truman

Our PRESIDENTS

President	Birthplace	Life Span	Presidency	Political Party	First Lady
Dwight D. Eisenhower	Texas	1890–1969	1953–1961	Republican	Mary "Mamie" Doud Eisenhower
John F. Kennedy	Massachusetts	1917–1963	1961–1963	Democrat	Jacqueline Bouvier Kennedy
Lyndon B. Johnson	Texas	1908–1973	1963–1969	Democrat	Claudia Alta Taylor Johnson
Richard M. Nixon	California	1913–1994	1969–1974	Republican	Thelma Catherine Ryan Nixon
Gerald Ford	Nebraska	1913–	1974–1977	Republican	Elizabeth "Betty" Bloomer Warren Ford
James Carter	Georgia	1924–	1977–1981	Democrat	Rosalynn Smith Carter
Ronald Reagan	Illinois	1911–	1981–1989	Republican	Nancy Davis Reagan
George Bush	Massachusetts	1924–	1989–1993	Republican	Barbara Pierce Bush
William Clinton	Arkansas	1946–	1993–2001	Democrat	Hillary Rodham Clinton
George W. Bush	Connecticut	1946–	2001–	Republican	Laura Welch Bush

Qualifications
To run for president, a candidate must
- be at least 35 years old
- be a citizen who was born in the United States
- have lived in the United States for 14 years

Term of Office
A president's term of office is four years. No president can stay in office for more than two terms.

Election Date
The presidential election takes place every four years on the first Tuesday of November.

Inauguration Date
Presidents are inaugurated on January 20.

Oath of Office
I do solemnly swear I will faithfully execute the office of the President of the United States and will to the best of my ability preserve, protect, and defend the Constitution of the United States.

Write a Letter to the President
One of the best things about being a U.S. citizen is that Americans get to participate in their government. They can speak out if they feel government leaders aren't doing their jobs. They can also praise leaders who are going the extra mile. Do you have something you'd like the president to do? Should the president worry more about the environment and encourage people to recycle? Should the government spend more money on our schools? You can write a letter to the president to say how you feel!

1600 Pennsylvania Avenue
Washington, D.C. 20500

You can even send an e-mail to: president@whitehouse.gov

For Further INFORMATION

Internet Sites

Visit Montpelier:
http://www.montpelier.org

Read a short biography of James Madison:
http://www.montpelier.org/hi-mad.html

Read some of James Madison's notes and letters:
http://www.virginia.edu/pjm

Visit the James Madison Museum:
http://www.gemlink.com/~jmmuseum

Learn more about the War of 1812:
http://www.cfcsc.dnd.ca/links/milhist/1812.html

Learn more about the Star-Spangled Banner:
http://americanhistory.si.edu/ssb/2_home/fs2.html

Learn more about all the presidents and visit the White House:
http://www.whitehouse.gov/WH/glimpse/presidents/html/presidents.html
http://www.thepresidency.org/presinfo.htm
http://www.americanpresidents.org/

Books

Fritz, Jean. *The Great Little Madison*. New York: Putnam, 1989.

Jones, Rebecca. *The Biggest (And Best) Flag That Ever Flew*. Centreville, MD: Tidewater Publishers, 1994.

Pflueger, Lynda. *Dolley Madison: Courageous First Lady* (Historical American Biographies). Springfield, NJ: Enslow Publishers, 1999.

Prolman, Marilyn. *The Constitution* (Cornerstones of Freedom). Danbury, CT: Childrens Press, 1995.

Robinet, Harriette Gillem. *Washington City Is Burning*. New York: Atheneum, 1996.

Stein, Richard Conrad. *The Bill of Rights* (Cornerstones of Freedom). Danbury, CT: Childrens Press, 1992.

Index

Adams, John, 18, 20
Alien Acts, 18, 20, 37
Articles of Confederation, 12–13, 36

Baltimore, 30, 35
Battle of New Orleans, 30
Bill of Rights, 16, 20, 37

checks and balances, 15
Church of England, 10
College of New Jersey, 7, 9, 36
Congress, 16
Constitution, U.S., 15, 36
Constitutional Convention, 14–15
Continental Congress, 11, 36

Declaration of Independence, 28
departments, of federal government, 16

Embargo Act, 23–25, 37
England, 7, 9, 17, 22–23, 26, 28–30, 32, 37
executive branch, 15

federal government, 12–16, 33
Federalist Papers, The, 17
Federalist Party, 17, 20, 27
Fort McHenry, 30, 35
France, 17, 22–23, 37
freedom of speech, 20

Hamilton, Alexander, 17
House of Representatives, 16, 36

Jackson, Andrew, 30
Jefferson, Thomas, 12, 16–17, 19–20, 22–24, 33, 37
judicial branch, 15

Key, Francis Scott, 35

legislative branch, 15

Madison, Dolley, 17–19, 21, 25–26, 28–29, 31–33, 37
Madison, James
  birth of, 6, 36
  childhood illnesses of, 6
  death of, 34, 37
  education of, 6–8, 36
  election of, 25, 37

inauguration of, 25
interest in politics, 10
law training of, 9–10
marriage of, 17–18, 37
reelection of, 28, 37
retirement of, 33–34
return to politics, 18, 36
as secretary of state, 22–24, 37
term in Congress, 12–13, 36
in Virginia legislature, 13, 36
work on U.S. Constitution, 14
Madison, James (father), 7
Madison, Nelly Conway, 33
Monroe, James, 31, 33, 37
Montpelier, 6, 9–10, 12, 18, 26, 32–33, 36–37

Perry, Oliver, 28
presidential mansion. *See* White House

religious freedom, 10–11
Republican Party, 17, 20
Revolutionary War, 10–11, 36
Roosevelt, Theodore, 30

Sedition Act, 18, 20, 37
slavery, 18
smugglers, 25
South Carolina, 33, 37
"Star-Spangled Banner, The," 35
states, trade agreements between, 13

Todd, Dolley Payne. *See* Madison, Dolley
trade, 22–25

Union, preservation of, 33–34
U.S.S. *Constitution,* 27

Virginia, constitution for, 11, 33–34, 37
Virginia Plan, 14
Virginia Revolutionary Convention, 11, 36

War of 1812, 26–32, 34, 37
Washington, D.C., 22, 28–29, 31, 35, 37
Washington, George, 15, 17–18
White House, 19, 26, 28, 30–31